Dragon's Hiccups

by Jenny Jinks and Martin Remphry

W
FRANKLIN WATTS
LONDON•SYDNEY

Dimpy the dragon had the hiccups –
dragon hiccups.

Every time she went "hic",
fire came out of her mouth.

Dimpy's friends wanted to help her.

Everyone went to Dimpy's house
for lunch.

Dimpy took the chips out of the oven.

"Yum!" she said.

But then ...

"Hic!" went Dimpy.

"Oh no!" everyone said.

So they all went to Sal's house
for lunch.

"Here you are," said Sal,
and she gave Dimpy some cake.

But then ...

"Hic!" went Dimpy.

"Oh no!" said Sal.

"Hold your breath," said Sal.

"That will stop the hiccups."

Dimpy held her breath.

Her face went red.

But then ...

"Hic!" went Dimpy.

Fire came out of her mouth again.

"Oh no!" said Sal. "My table!"

"We can get rid of your hiccups,"

said her friends.

"Close your eyes."

Dimpy closed her eyes.

When she opened them,

everyone had gone.

"No one wants to be

my friend," she said, sadly.

Everyone jumped out at Dimpy.

"BOO!" they shouted.

Dimpy jumped.

"Aaah!" she cried.

But then ...

"Hic!" went Dimpy

and fire came out of her mouth.

Her friends got out of the way,

just in time.

"It didn't work," said Dimpy.

13

Dimpy felt sad.

"I'm sorry," she said.

"You need to drink some water," said her friends.

Dimpy ran into the kitchen.

She put her head in the sink

and gulped down all the water.

Every last drop.

"Aaah, that's better," Dimpy said.

Everyone waited ...

... no hiccups.

Everyone looked at Dimpy.

They waited ... and waited.

"My hiccups have gone!" said Dimpy.

"Hooray!" shouted all her friends.

But then ...

"Hic!" went Dimpy.

Story order

Look at these 5 pictures and captions.
Put the pictures in the right order
to retell the story.

1

Dimpy set fire to the chips.

2

Dimpy blew bubbles.

3

Her friends tried to help.

4

Dimpy had dragon hiccups.

5

Dimpy drank lots of water.

21

Independent Reading

This series is designed to provide an opportunity for your child to read on their own. These notes are written for you to help your child choose a book and to read it independently.

In school, your child's teacher will often be using reading books which have been banded to support the process of learning to read. Use the book band colour your child is reading in school to help you make a good choice. *Dragon's Hiccups* is a good choice for children reading at Orange Band in their classroom to read independently.

The aim of independent reading is to read this book with ease, so that your child enjoys the story and relates it to their own experiences.

About the book

Dimpy the dragon has hiccups. She keeps setting fire to everything. Her friends try to help, but nothing seems to work. Then she drinks the water in the sink, and starts hiccuping bubbles instead of fire!

Before reading

Help your child to learn how to make good choices by asking:
"Why did you choose this book? Why do you think you will enjoy it?"
Look at the cover together and ask: "What do you think the story will be about?" Ask your child to think of what they already know about the story context. Then ask your child to read the title aloud.
Ask: "What do you know about dragons in stories? What do they usually breathe out?"
Remind your child that they can sound out the letters to make a word if they get stuck.
Decide together whether your child will read the story independently or read it aloud to you.

During reading

Remind your child of what they know and what they can do independently. If reading aloud, support your child if they hesitate or ask for help by telling the word. If reading to themselves, remind your child that they can come and ask for your help if stuck.

After reading

Support comprehension by asking your child to tell you about the story. Use the story order puzzle to encourage your child to retell the story in the right sequence, in their own words. The correct sequence can be found on the next page.

Help your child think about the messages in the book that go beyond the story and ask: "Would you like to have a dragon for a friend? Why/why not?"

Give your child a chance to respond to the story: "Did you have a favourite part? What do your friends try to help you with? What do you help your friends with?"

Extending learning

Help your child understand the story structure by using the same sentence patterning and adding different elements. "Let's make up a new story about a dragon with a problem. What is wrong with this dragon? What happens because of this problem? Can the problem be solved, and if so, how?"

In the classroom, your child's teacher may be teaching how to use speech marks to show when characters are speaking.

There are many examples in this book that you could look at with your child. Find these together and point out how the end punctuation (comma, full stop or exclamation mark) comes inside the speech mark.

Franklin Watts
First published in Great Britain in 2017
by The Watts Publishing Group

Series Editors: Jackie Hamley and Melanie Palmer
Series Advisors: Dr Sue Bodman and Glen Franklin
Series Designer: Peter Scoulding

A CIP catalogue record for this book is
available from the British Library.

ISBN 978 1 4451 5351 3 (hbk)
ISBN 978 1 4451 5352 0 (pbk)
ISBN 978 1 4451 6100 6 (library ebook)

Printed in China

Franklin Watts
An imprint of
Hachette Children's Group
Part of The Watts Publishing Group
Carmelite House
50 Victoria Embankment
London EC4Y 0DZ

An Hachette UK Company
www.hachette.co.uk

www.franklinwatts.co.uk

FSC
www.fsc.org
MIX
Paper from
responsible sources
FSC® C104740

Answer to Story order: 4, 1, 3, 5, 2